LEVERKUSEN

DIE SCHÖNSTEN SEITEN | AT ITS BEST

Im Japanischen Garten der Bayer AG. In the Bayer AG Japanese Garden.

Detlef Braun

LEVERKUSEN

DIE SCHÖNSTEN SEITEN

AT ITS BEST

SUTTON
VERLAG

Impressum

Sutton Verlag GmbH
Hochheimer Straße 59
99094 Erfurt
http://www.suttonverlag.de
Copyright © Sutton Verlag, 2012

ISBN: 978-3-86680-970-3
Gestaltung und Satz: Sutton Verlag
Übersetzung: tolingo GmbH, Hamburg
Druck: Europrint a.s., Prag, Tschechische Republik

Vom Dorf zur Großstadt | From Village to City　　　　　　　6

Bayer und Leverkusen | Bayer and Leverkusen　　　　　　　7

Wiesdorf　　　　　　　16

Manfort　　　　　　　25

Küppersteg　　　　　　　26

Bürrig　　　　　　　31

Opladen　　　　　　　34

Alkenrath　　　　　　　42

Schlebusch　　　　　　　46

Steinbüchel　　　　　　　52

Rheindorf　　　　　　　56

Hitdorf　　　　　　　62

Quettingen　　　　　　　70

Bergisch Neukirchen　　　　　　　72

Lützenkirchen　　　　　　　77

Dank | Acknowledgements　　　　　　　79

Die kreisfreie Stadt Leverkusen besteht nicht, wie Fremde vermuten mögen, aus Chemiefabriken, Einkaufszonen, Bayer 04, dem Autobahnkreuz und einem Multiplex-Kino, sondern aus 13 ehemals selbstständigen, zumeist sehr schön gelegenen Ortsteilen mit rund 161.000 Einwohnern. Die Stadt verfügt über eine hervorragende Verkehrsinfrastruktur zwischen den Metropolen Köln und Düsseldorf. 2012 soll eine Verkehrsleitzentrale eingerichtet werden, die den Verkehr auf den Autobahnen des Landes überwachen und lenken soll.

Orte wie Steinbüchel, Quettingen, Rheindorf und Hitdorf haben sich ihren dörflichen Charakter großenteils bewahrt. Leverkusen ist eine Drei-Flüsse-Stadt. Diverse Hochwasserschutzanlagen schirmen den Ort vor dem Hochwasser des Rheins, der Wupper und der Dhünn ab. Für den Schutz der eigenen Grundstücke ist jedoch jeder Bürger selbst zuständig. In Rheindorf mündet die Wupper in den Rhein, nachdem sie kurz zuvor die Dhünn aufgenommen hat.

Das Wappen der Stadt zeigt einen blaugekrönten, zweischwänzigen, aufsteigenden roten Bergischen Löwen vor einem silbernen Hintergrund, davor einen schwarzen Wechselzinnenbalken. Der Löwe ist von alters her das Wappentier der Grafen und Herzöge von Berg. Wiesdorf, Schlebusch, Steinbüchel und Rheindorf wurden am 1. April 1930 zusammengeschlossen. Als Name der größeren Stadt wurde die seit 1862 gebräuchliche Bezeichnung der Werkssiedlung Leverkusen gewählt.

Bei der Kommunalen Gebietsreform am 1. Januar 1975 wurden Leverkusen, die Kreisstadt Opladen sowie die Stadt Bergisch Neukirchen zu einer neuen kreisfreien Stadt zusammengeschlossen und das zu Monheim gehörende Hitdorf in diese eingegliedert. Namensgeber der Stadt ist der 1804 in Wermelskirchen geborene Chemiker und Unternehmer Carl Leverkus. Er gründete dort 1834 die erste Fabrik zur Herstellung von künstlichem Ultramarinblau. Später verlegte er seine Fabrik nach Wiesdorf. Die neu entstandene Siedlung nannte er *Leverkusen*.

Bergisch Gladbach, im Februar 2012
Detlef Braun

Whatever outsiders may think, there is more to the self-governing city of Leverkusen than chemical factories, shopping zones, Bayer 04, the motorway junction and a multiplex cinema. In actual fact the city is comprised of 13 former independent villages and is home to 161,000 inhabitants. The city has excellent transportation facilities providing access to the metropolises of Cologne and Düsseldorf. In 2012 a traffic control centre is to be set up to monitor and guide the traffic on the motorways.

Places such as Steinbüchel, Quettingen, Rheindorf and Hitdorf have to a large extent retained their village-like character. Leverkusen is a city of three rivers. Various flood control installations protect the city from flood waters from the Rhine, the Wupper and the Dhünn. However, the inhabitants are responsible for protecting their own property. Just after the Dhünn flows into the Wupper, the Wupper itself flows into the Rhine in Rheindorf.

Leverkusen's coat of arms depicts a rampant red Bergisch lion with two tails and a blue crown against a silver background in front of a black embattled line. From time immemorial the lion has been the heraldic emblem of the counts and dukes of Berg.

On 1 April 1930 Wiesdorf, Schlebusch, Steinbüchel and Rheindorf were merged to form one large town. The name of the larger town was taken from the name for the company housing estate "Leverkusen" which had been in existence since 1862.

In the local government redivision on 1 January 1975 Leverkusen, the district capital Opladen, the town of Bergisch Neukirchen and Hitdorf – up to then part of Monheim – were merged into a new self-governing city.

The name of the city can be traced back to the chemist and entrepreneur Carl Leverkus who was born in Wermelskirchen in 1804. In 1834 he founded the first factory to manufacture artificial ultramarine blue dye. Later on he moved his factory to Wiesdorf and named the newly built workers estate *Leverkusen*.

Bergisch Gladbach, February 2012
Detlef Braun

Bayer als größter Arbeitgeber am Standort Leverkusen hat die Stadt nachhaltig geprägt. Besonders im Bereich des Wohnungsbaus, des Sports und der sozialen Belange seiner Mitarbeiter hat der Chemie-riese Vorbildliches geleistet.
Auf dem Firmengelände steht auch das von 1903 bis 1912 erbaute ehemalige Hauptverwaltungsgebäude. An seiner Fassade befinden sich Reliefs des Düsseldorfer Bildhauers Joseph (Job) Hammerschmidt (1873–1926). Im Giebel ist eine allegorische Darstellung der Chemie (weiblich) und der Technik (männlich). Im Sockelgeschoss befanden sich zwölf Monatsbilder, von denen noch acht erhalten sind.

As the largest employer in Leverkusen, Bayer has really made its mark on the city. Particularly in the areas of housing, sports and the social interests of its staff, the che-mical giant has been a real role model.
The former main administration building – built between 1903 and 1912 – is still located in the grounds of the company. The facade features reliefs carved by the Düsseldorf sculptor Joseph "Job" Hammer-schmidt (1873–1926). On the gable there is an allegoric depiction of chemistry (female) and tech-nology (male). In the basement there used to be 12 labours of the month of which eight remain.

Der CHEMPARK ist mit Standorten in Leverkusen, Dormagen und Krefeld-Uerdingen der größte Chemiepark Deutschlands. In mehr als 70 dort angesiedelten Firmen sind über 46.000 Mitarbeiter beschäftigt. Auf dem Wiesdorfer Gelände befinden sich Verwaltung und Produktionsstätten des Bayer-Konzerns (Chemie, Pharma, Landwirtschaft) sowie der Lanxess AG (Spezialchemikalien, Kunststoffe, Kautschuke).

With sites in Leverkusen, Dormagen and Krefeld-Uerdingen, CHEMPARK is the largest chemical park in Germany. Over 70 companies are located there and they employ over 46,000 members of staff. The administration facilities and the production halls of both the Bayer Group (chemical, pharmaceutical and agriculture) and Lanxess AG (special chemicals, synthetics and rubber) are located on the Wiesdorf site.

Blick auf Leverkusen mit dem CHEMPARK in Wiesdorf, 2011.
A view of Leverkusen and CHEMPARK in Wiesdorf, 2011.

Werkseingang Tor I (Pförtner I) an der B8. *Factory entrance gate I (gatekeeper I) on the B8.*

Die Bayer AG baute von Ende des 19. Jahrhunderts bis Anfang des 20. Jahrhunderts in mehreren Ortsteilen Wohnhäuser für ihre Mitarbeiter, sogenannte Kolonien. Die mit einfachen Wohnhäusern ausgestattete Kolonie I besteht nicht mehr. Kolonie II enthält malerisch gestaltete Einzelbauten, während Kolonie III mehr städtebaulich angelegt wurde. Außerdem gab es eine Eigenheimkolonie. Für leitende Angestellte wurden Miet-Villen in Werksnähe zwischen der heutigen B8 und der Eisenbahnlinie gebaut.
Wer sich für die Geschichte der Bayer-Kolonien interessiert, erfährt mehr hierzu im Kolonie-Museum an der Nobelstraße 78–82.

From the end of the 19th to the beginning of the 20th century, Bayer AG built houses for its workers in many different villages. These were known as colonies. Colony I, which featured simple houses, no longer exists. Colony II features artistically designed detached houses while Colony III is built in a more urban style. In addition to this there is also a colony of private residential buildings. Rental villas were built near the plant between the train lines and what is now the B8 for managers.
If you are interested in finding out more about the Bayer housing colonies, visit the Colony Museum at Nobelstraße 78–82.

Wohnhäuser und Kolonie-Museum an der Nobelstraße. Houses and the Colony Museum on Nobelstraße.

Ein Juwel ist der kunstvoll gestaltete, gepflegte Japanische Garten der Bayer AG an der Kaiser-Wilhelm-Allee in Wiesdorf. Er wurde 1913 angelegt und von Carl Duisberg nach einer Weltreise bedeutend erweitert. Wegen knapper und reservierter Parkplätze empfiehlt sich der Besuch am Wochenende.

A jewel in the Bayer crown is the artistically designed, well-tended Japanese Garden in Kaiser-Wilhelm-Allee in Wiesdorf. It was laid out in 1913 and significantly extended by Carl Duisberg after he returned from a world tour. Due to a lack of parking spaces, many of which are reserved, it is best to visit at the weekend.

Im Japanischen Garten. In the Japanese Garden.

Im September 2011 fand auf dem Flugplatz Kurtekotten des Luftsportclubs Bayer Leverkusen das alljährliche Flugplatzfest statt. Sportmaschinen und Modellflugzeuge vollführten spannende Kunstflüge, und für das leibliche Wohl der Zuschauer war bestens gesorgt.

In September 2011 the annual air field fete took place at Kurtekotten air field, home of Luftsportclub Bayer Leverkusen. Sporting aircraft and model aeroplanes executed exciting aerobatics, and a range of food and drinks was provided for the spectators.

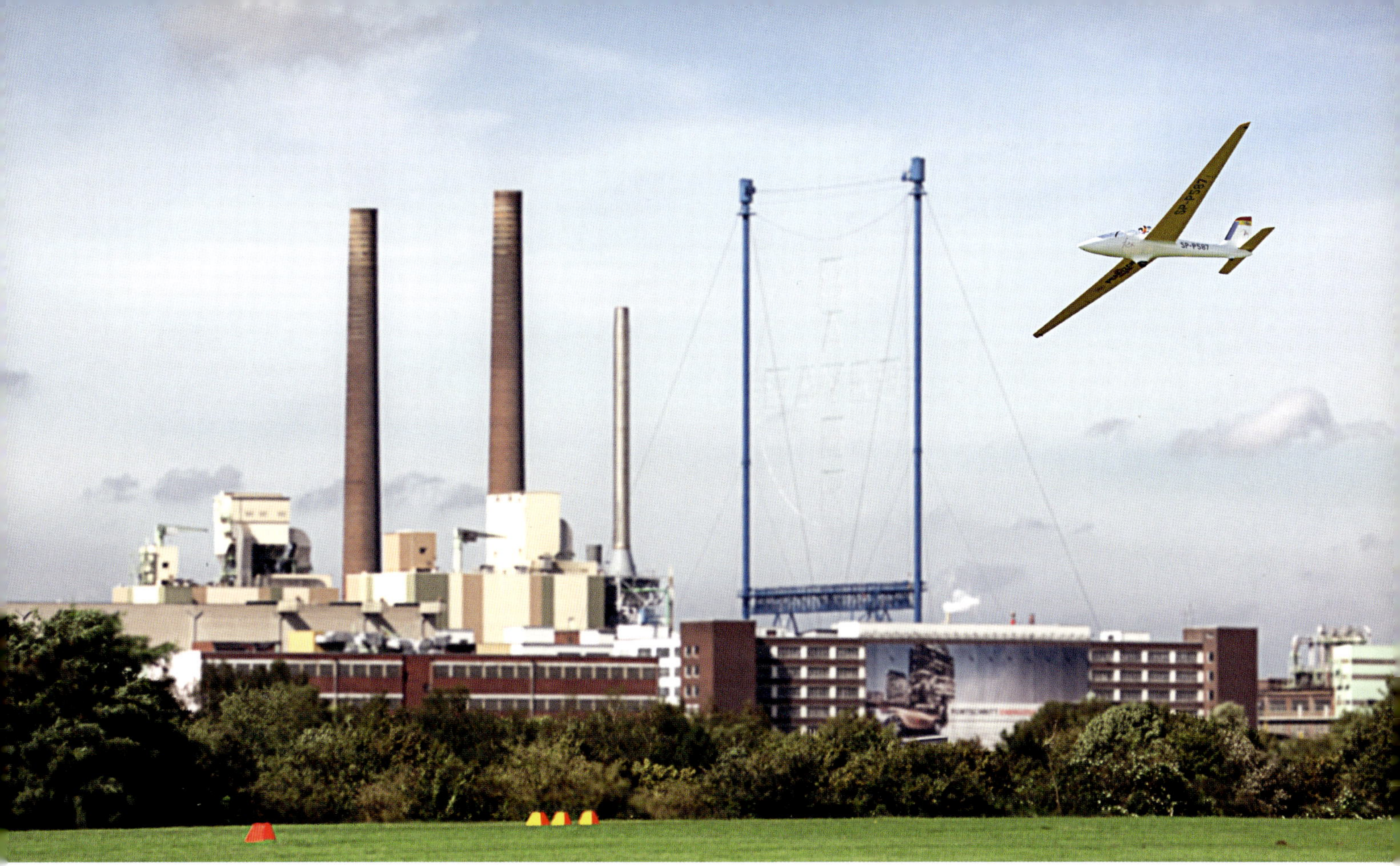
SP-P587
SP-P587

HERZLICH WILLKOMMEN

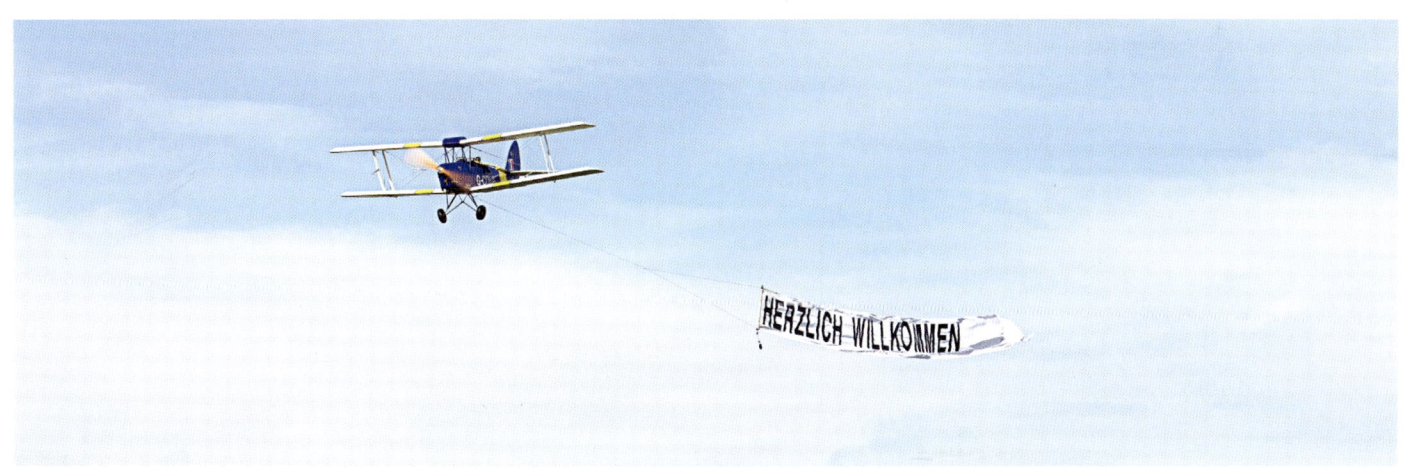

In Wiesdorf schlägt das Herz Leverkusens. Hier eilen die Menschen durch die zahlreichen Geschäfte, wird die Stadt verwaltet, finden kulturelle Veranstaltungen statt. Das Zentrum lag ursprünglich unmittelbar am Rhein und wurde von dessen Fluten wiederholt heimgesucht. Im Jahr 1571 veränderte der Fluss seinen Lauf, zerstörte Häuser und die Kirche. Nach einem verheerenden weiteren Hochwasser anno 1657 wurde das Dorf weiter östlich wieder aufgebaut.

Martin Luthers Kirchenlied „Ein feste Burg ist unser Gott" ist der Wahlspruch der monumentalen evangelischen Christuskirche von 1906. Sie wurde 1944 durch Bomben zerstört, 1948/1949 wieder aufgebaut und 2001 gründlich renoviert. In der Kirche wurde 1934 der Leverkusener Bildhauer Kurt Arentz getauft.

Im überdachten „City Center" wurden die darin angesiedelten Einzelhandelsgeschäfte und Kaufhäuser vor der Eröffnung der „Rathaus Galerie" (Seite 18) sehr gut angenommen, zumal sich dort eine Tiefgarage befindet.

Inzwischen ist es im „City Center" ruhiger geworden, denn seit 2010 sind viele Firmen in die „Rathaus Galerie", gleich nebenan, umgezogen. Das Center teilt damit das Schicksal anderer traditioneller Läden in Orten mit hypermodernen Konsumtempeln.

Evangelische Christuskirche.
Evangelical Christuskirche
(church of Christ).

The heart of Leverkusen beats in Wiesdorf. This is where people shop, the city is run and cultural events take place. The centre was originally situated close to the Rhine but was constantly plagued by flooding. In 1571 the river changed course, destroying numerous houses and the church. After another devastating flood in around 1657 the village was relocated further east.

Martin Luther's hymn "A Mighty Fortress Is Our God" is the motto of the monumental Evangelical Christuskirche, built in 1906. The church was destroyed by Allied bombing in 1944 but was rebuilt in 1948/1949. In 2001 it was completely renovated. The Leverkusen sculptor Kurt Arentz was christened here in 1934.

Before the opening of the Rathaus Galerie (see page 18) the numerous retailers and shops in the City Center shopping arcade were well catered for, particularly as it had an underground car park.

Nowadays the City Center shopping arcade is a lot quieter, as many shops moved next door into the Rathaus Galerie in 2010. The arcade thus shares the fate of other traditional shops in towns with temples dedicated to modern-day consumerism.

Im „City Center".
In the "City Center".

Im Februar 2010 eröffnete die futuristische „Rathaus Galerie" in Wiesdorf. Über einem Einkaufszentrum mit rund 22.600 Quadratmetern Verkaufsfläche, Dienstleistungs- und Gastronomiebetrieben, arbeitet die Stadtverwaltung in einer verglasten Rotunde mit rund 5.000 Quadratmetern Bürofläche.

In February 2010 the futuristic "Rathaus Galerie" opened in Wiesdorf. The shopping centre features around 22,600 m^2 for shops, service providers and eateries. Above it all the city administration offices are housed in a glazed rotunda with office space of 5,000 m^2.

Die „Rathaus Galerie". *The "Rathaus Galerie".*

Impressionen vom Wiesdorfer Weihnachtsmarkt 2011. Wetterkapriolen bescherten dem Rheinland eine relativ milde Weihnachtszeit.

Pictures of the Wiesdorf Christmas market 2011. Freak weather conditions meant that the Rhineland had a relatively mild Christmas time that year.

Am Büchelter Hof, vom Einkaufs-
zentrum durch den Europaring (die
B8) getrennt, liegt das Forum, der
Veranstaltungsort für Theaterauf-
führungen und Konzerte, Kongresse,
Tagungen und Bälle. Dort ist auch die
Volkshochschule angesiedelt. Das
von Ulrich von Altenstadt geplante
Gebäude bildete 1969 den ersten
Abschnitt der neuen City Wiesdorf.
Der Theatersaal fasst 1.000, der
Agamsaal 800 Menschen.

Separated from the shopping centre
by the Europaring (B8) is the Forum
at Büchelter Hof. This is where plays,
concerts, meetings, conferences and
balls take place. You can also find
the adult education college here.
The building, designed by Ulrich von
Altenstadt in 1969, formed the first
section of the new city of Wiesdorf.
The theatre can hold 1,000 spectators, and the Agamsaal 800.

Im Jahr 2005 fand in Wiesdorf die Landesgartenschau auf einer an den Rhein angrenzenden ehemaligen Deponie statt, die zuvor mit Planen und einer zusätzlichen Erdschicht abgedeckt wurde. Der hier entstandene Neuland-Park mit seinen Themengärten, Spielplätzen, Bänken und Liegen ist sehr familienfreundlich und wird gut angenommen.
Jeweils am 3. Adventswochenende wird der Nordische Weihnachtsmarkt mit seinen typischen rot-weißen Schwedenhäuschen abgehalten.

In 2005 the State Horticultural Show took place in Wiesdorf on a former landfill site next to the Rhine. The preliminary work involved covering the site with tarpaulins and an additional layer of soil. The site was then turned into Neuland Park. It features themed gardens, play areas, benches and sun loungers. The park is very family friendly and was well received by the public.
On the third weekend of advent the Scandinavian Christmas market, with its typical red and white huts, takes place here.

Lebendige und hölzerne Radler.
Real and lifelike wooden cyclists.

Die Doktorsburg 2011. "Doktorsburg" in 2011.

Die im Wiesdorfer Stadtpark idyllisch gelegene Doktorsburg von 1682 ist ein Teil des früheren Büchelter Hofes. Sie ist nach dem Titel des Dr. Jakob von Omphal benannt, der das Grundstück 1540 erwarb. Ursprünglich war die Doktorsburg eine Wasserburg, gespeist vom aus der Dhünn abgeleiteten Mühlbach und dem Mutzbach, der jetzt unterirdisch in die Dhünn fließt. Heute ist sie ein „Haus der älteren Bürger".

Doktorsburg dates back to 1682 and is part of the former Büchelter Hof. It has an idyllic location in Wiesdorf Park. The house is named after Dr. Jakob von Omphal who bought the property in 1540. Originally Doktorsburg was a moated castle which was fed by diverting the streams Mühlbach and Mutzbach from the river Dhünn. The Mutzbach now returns to the Dhünn underground. Today the house provides facilities for senior citizens.

Die Doktorsburg um 1846. "Doktorsburg" in around 1846.

Pfarrkirche St. Joseph.
Parish church St. Joseph.

Wiesdorf geht in Manfort über. Der Name kommt von einer Stelle im Rhein, die ein Mann durchwaten konnte („Mannesfurt").
Als Wahrzeichen des Ortes gilt die markante katholische Pfarrkirche St. Joseph von 1913. Sehenswert ist auch der 1936/37 erbaute Lindenhof in der Weiherstraße, dessen ursprüngliche Bebauung bis in die 1870er-Jahre zurückgeht.

Wiesdorf eventually turns into Manfort. The name comes from a part of the Rhine which was shallow enough for a man could wade through – "Man's ford".
One landmark is the impressive Catholic parish church of St. Joseph, built in 1913. Also worth seeing is the Lindenhof building. It was completed in 1936/37 but can trace its roots back to the 1870s.

Christus-König-Pfarrkirche. Christus-König parish church.

Den bereits 1157 als „Steg über die Dhünn" bei Bürrig erwähnten Ort durchschneidet heute der tiefliegende, vierspurige Europaring (die B8) in einen östlichen und einen westlichen Teil. Die dort gelegene Christus-König-Kirche wurde 1928 nach Plänen von Dominikus Böhm erbaut.

Mentioned as early as 1157 as the "bridge over the Dhünn" near Bürrig, modern-day Küppersteg intersects the four-lane, low lying Europaring (B8) and is split into an east end and a west end. The Christus-König parish church was built here in 1928 according to plans drawn by Dominikus Böhm.

BayArena, Stadion von Bayer 04 Leverkusen. BayArena, stadium of Bayer 04 Leverkusen.

Die BayArena in Küppersteg ist das Stadion von Bayer 04 Leverkusen. Mit gut 30.000 Plätzen gehört die Sportstätte zu den kleineren Stadien. Sie liegt nicht wie üblich außerhalb, sondern mitten in der Stadt. Das Verkehrsproblem löste man durch ein Shuttlebus-System zwischen dem CHEMPARK-Parkplatz Kurtekotten und dem Stadion.

The BayArena in Küppersteg is the home of Bayer 04 Leverkusen. With some 30,000 seats, the stadium is one of the smallest of its kind. Unlike most football stadiums it is not located out of town but, instead, right in the middle. The transportation problems are solved by a shuttle bus system between the CHEMPARK car park Kurtekotten and the stadium.

Die Mesxhidi-Aksa-Moschee der Albanischen Gemeinde in Leverkusen wurde 2005 fertiggestellt. Der Imam (Vorbeter) erklärte mir die Inneneinrichtung:

Ganz vorn befindet sich die in Richtung zur Kaaba zeigende Gebetsnische, der Mihrab (1). Von dort leitet der Imam das Gebet der Gemeinde. Rechts daneben befindet sich ein hoher Predigerplatz, der Minbar (2). Er wird freitags nach der Predigt zwischen dem selbstständigen und dem gemeinsamen Gebet genutzt. Links vom Mihrab steht eine kleine Kanzel, der Kursi (3). Ebenso wie der Mihrab ist auch der Gebetsteppich nach Mekka ausgerichtet. Auf ihm beten die Männer, während die Frauen im Obergeschoss Allah verehren. Für den praktizierenden Muslim sei die Zeit wichtig, weil er verpflichtet sei, fünfmal täglich zu beten, erläuterte der Imam weiter. Deshalb zeige eine Standuhr die Zeit an.

In 2005 the Mesxhidi-Aksa mosque for the Albanian community was completed. The imam (prayer leader) explained the interior to me:

At the front facing towards Mecca is the prayer niche, the mihrab (1). This is where the imam stands to lead the prayers. On the right next to the mihrab is a raised pulpit known as the minbar (2). It is used on Fridays after the sermon between the independent and communal prayers. To the left of the mihrab is a smaller pulpit, the kursi (3). As in the mihrab, the prayer mat is orientated towards Mecca. This is where the men pray while the women pray upstairs. For practising Muslims, time is important as it is compulsory to pray five times a day, explains the imam. That is why there is also a grandfather clock in the mosque.

Im Wildpark Reuschenberg finden die Besucher heimische Wild- und Haustierarten sowie einige vom Aussterben bedrohte Tiere vor.

In the wild animal park Reuschenberg you will come across local wild and domesticated animals as well as certain endangered species.

Bienenhaus, Stachelschweine, Ziegenfütterung. *Bee hive, porcupines, goats being fed.*

Wasserturm in Bürrig. Water tower in Bürrig.

Der weithin sichtbare Bürriger EVL-Wasserturm ist eines der Leverkusener Wahrzeichen. Im Jahr 1974 geplant und 1978 fertiggestellt, dient das 73 Meter hohe Bauwerk an der Olof-Palme-Straße mit einem Behälterdurchmesser von 42 Metern auch als Aussichtsplattform. Beide Kammern fassen 4.000 Kubikmeter. Der Schaft misst im Durchmesser acht Meter. Von oben hat man einen Rundum-Blick auf Leverkusen und die Nachbarstadt Köln. Bei klarer Sicht schaut man sogar bis zum Siebengebirge.

The EVL water tower in Bürrig can be seen from miles around and is a real Leverkusen landmark. Planned in 1974 and completed in 1978, the 73-metre-high tower on Olof-Palme-Straße has a container with a diameter of 42 metres and also serves as a viewing platform. Both chambers hold 4,000 cubic metres of water. The shaft is eight metres in diameter. From above there is a brilliant view of Leverkusen and the neighbouring city of Cologne. When the weather is clear it is even possible to see as far as the Siebengebirge mountains.

Die Reuschenberger Mühle von 1477 bzw. 1847 (Jahr der Erneuerung) wurde früher als Korn-, Öl-, Loh- und Papiermühle genutzt. Heute erzeugen zwei Turbinen Strom aus der Kraft der Wupper. Ein idyllischer Weg führt am Mühlengraben entlang zum Tierheim in Opladen.

The Reuschenberger Mill dates back to 1477 (it was renovated in 1847) and was previously used as a corn mill, an oil mill, a bark mill and a paper mill. Today the two turbines produce electricity using the power of the river Wupper. An idyllic path leads along the mill stream to the animal shelter in Opladen.

Überlauf des Wupper-Müh-
lengrabens der Reuschen-
berger Mühle.
The flooded Wupper mill
stream belonging to the
Reuschenberger mill.

Wupper-Mühlengraben der
Reuschenberger Mühle.
The Wupper mill stream
belonging to the Reuschen-
berger mill.

Auf dem Gelände des Ende 2003 geschlossenen Eisenbahnaus-besserungswerks Opladen wird im Rahmen der „Regionale 2010" das Projekt „neue bahn stadt:opladen" verwirklicht. Es entsteht ein attraktiver Stadtteil mit Wohnungen, Gewerbe- und Dienst-leistungsbetrieben sowie der Fachhochschule „Campus Lever-kusen". Letztere gehört zur Fachhochschule Köln und soll den Lehrbetrieb 2013 aufnehmen.

Im Zentrum der früheren Kreisstadt steht St. Remigius, eine der ältesten Pfarreien Leverkusens. Die Kirche wurde erstmals 1123 in einer Urkunde des Kölner Stifts St. Gereon erwähnt. Im Jahr 1862 wurde sie abgerissen und neu erbaut. Bei einem Bomben-angriff am 28. Dezember 1944 wurde St. Remigius bis auf die Außenmauern und den Turm zerstört. Von 1945 bis 1952 erfolgte der Wiederaufbau mit Hilfe der Gemeindemitglieder.

In der Fußgängerzone wird alljährlich ein Weihnachtsmarkt abgehalten, das „Bergische Dorf". In mehr als 30 Fachwerkhäus-chen finden die Besucher allerlei Weihnachtliches wie Schmuck, Bastelbedarf und Naschwerk.

Pfarrkirche St. Remigius um 1860.
Parish church St. Remigius in around 1860.

On the site of the old Opladen railway repair plant, which closed at the end of 2003, a new project called "neue bahn stadt: opladen" (new rail town opladen) is being implemented as part of "Regionale 2010". The project will create an attractive new quar-ter with apartments, businesses and service providers as well as the Leverkusen campus of the Cologne University of Applied Sciences. The latter is due to open in 2013.

In the centre of the former district capital is the church of St. Remigius, the oldest parish in Leverkusen. The church was first mentioned in 1123 in a deed belonging to the Cologne-based foundation of St. Gereon. In 1862 the church was torn down and rebuilt. During a bombing raid on 28 December 1944, St. Remi-gius was totally destroyed save for the external walls and the tower. With the help of the community it was rebuilt from 1945 to 1952.

The annual Bergisches Village Christmas market is held in the pedestrian area. In over 30 little huts, visitors can find all sorts of Christmassy things, such as jewellery and decorations, craft supplies and snacks.

◄ *Pfarrkirche St. Remigius 2011. Parish church St. Remigius in 2011.* ►

Aloysiuskapelle.
Aloysius chapel.

Die katholische Aloysiuskapelle, ehemals Teil des Aloysianums, steht am Ende der Opladener Fußgängerzone/ Opladener Platz.
Letzteres war von 1850 bis 1938 ein Gymnasium des Erzbistums Köln. Der Schulkomplex diente ab 1939 als Opladener Rathaus und Berufsschule. Nach der Kommunalen Gebietsreform 1975 wurde das Aloysianum bis auf die Kapelle abgerissen. Diese wird seit 1995 als eine der ersten Jugendkirchen genutzt.

The Catholic Aloysius chapel, formerly part of the Aloysianum, is located at the end of the pedestrian area/Opladener Platz.
From 1850 to 1938, the latter was a grammar school belonging to the archdiocese of Cologne. From 1939 the school became the Opladen town hall and a vocational school. After the local government reorganisation in 1975 the Aloysianum was torn down but the chapel was left standing. This has since 1995 been used as one of the first youth churches.

In der Fußgängerzone. ▶
In the pedestrian area.

Hotel „Villa Fürstenberg" am Fürstenberg Platz. Hotel "Villa Fürstenberg" on Fürstenberg Platz.

Die ehemalige Weskott'sche Villa vom Anfang des 20. Jahrhunderts wurde 2006 an Duisburger Investoren verkauft, die sie zum Hotel „Villa Fürstenberg" umbauen ließen. Sie dient weiterhin auch als Stadthalle.

Der Friedenberger Hof ist die Zentrale des Bundes der historischen Deutschen Schützenbruderschaften e.V. Der Rittersitz aus dem 14./15. Jahrhundert wurde entkernt und modernisiert. Von der alten Innenausstattung blieben nur Dachbalken und Treppe übrig.

The former Weskott'sche Villa, which dates back to the early 20th century, was sold in 2006 to Duisburg investors, who transformed it into Hotel "Villa Fürstenberg". It also still functions as the town hall.

Friedenberger Hof is the home of the Bund der historischen Deutschen Schützenbruderschaften e.V. (Association of Historic German Rifle Clubs). The 14th/15th century knights' manor was gutted and modernised. Of the old interior fittings only the roof beams and the stairs remained.

Friedenberger Hof, Schützenvogel im Hausflur.
"Friedenberger Hof". The "Schützenvogel" (a wooden
bird – often called "eagle" –, at which members of
rifle clubs shoot during their annual rifle club festival)
can be found in the hallway.

Die Villa Römer aus dem Jahr 1905 ist ein Beispiel großbürgerlicher Repräsentationsarchitektur. Zur Anlage gehört ein Park im englischen Landschaftsstil mit Brunnen, dem Kutscherhaus und einer (nicht mehr vorhandenen) Orangerie. Seit Ende 2011 beherbergt die Villa die erste Dauerausstellung zur Stadtgeschichte Leverkusens.

Villa Römer, built in 1905, is an example of prestigious upper-class architecture. The property included an English country garden with fountains, the coach house and an orangery which no longer exists. Since the end of 2011 the villa has been housing the first permanent exhibition on the history of Leverkusen.

Villa Römer, Kutscherhaus.
"Villa Römer", coachman's house.

Ehemaliges Landratsamt. *Former District Office.*

Das 1914 erbaute ehemalige Landratsamt des Rhein-Wupper-Kreises beherbergt heute das Leverkusener Stadtarchiv. In dem Gebäude wohnte früher auch der Landrat.

The former District Office of the Rhine-Wupper district was built in 1914 and today houses the Leverkusen city archive. The District Administrator also used to live in the building.

In Alkenrath liegt das schon 1328 als „Burg" erwähnte majestätische Schloss Morsbroich in einem weitläufigen Park. Es war von 1619 bis 1803 Sitz des Deutschen Ritterordens. Im Jahr 1774 ließ Ignaz von Roll die verfallene Burg abbauen und an ihrer Stelle ein barockes Schlösschen errichten. Um diese Zeit wurde auch der Englische Garten angelegt. Das Schloss wurde 1885 um zwei Flügel erweitert. Nachdem die Stadt Leverkusen Gebäude und Park 1974 erwarb, beherbergt Morsbroich seit 1985 ein Museum für zeitgenössische Kunst.

In Alkenrath you can find the majestic Morsbroich castle set in a spacious park. The building was mentioned as early as 1328 and was referred to as a "castle". From 1619 until 1803 it was the headquarters of the Teutonic Knights. In 1774 Ignaz von Roll knocked down the derelict castle and built a Baroque palace in its place. It was during this period that the English garden was laid out. In 1885 the palace was extended with two new wings. The city of Leverkusen acquired the building and the park in 1974, and since 1985 it has been a museum of contemporary art.

Kunstobjekte im Park Morsbroich.
Sculptures in Morsbroich Park.

Schloss Morsbroich. Morsbroich castle.

Glasobjekt am Schloss.
A glass object at the palace.

Junge Graureiher am Alkenrather Weiher.
Young grey herons at Alkenrath pond.

Der Schäfer Gezelinus entdeckte um 1135 eine Quelle, der man später eine heilkräftige Wirkung nachsagte. Nach seinem Tode errichtete man über der Quelle eine Kapelle, zu der die Gläubigen bei Wallfahrten pilgerten. Das hölzerne Gebäude wurde später durch einen Ziegelsteinbau ersetzt.

In 1135 a shepherd named Gezelinus discovered a spring, which later on was said to have healing properties. After his death a chapel was built over the spring and is now a pilgrimage destination. The original wooden building was later replaced with a brick one.

Der Inhaber der ARAL-Tankstelle an der Alkenrather Straße hat offensichtlich ein Faible für alte Fluggeräte. Seit 2005 steht auf seinem Grundstück ein russischer Antonov Doppeldecker AN 2. Im Oktober 2011 gesellte sich ein nach russischem Patent in Polen gebauter Hubschrauber MIL-MI-2 hinzu.

The owner of the ARAL petrol station on Alkenrather Straße seems to have a penchant for old aircraft. Since 2005 an old Russian Antonov double-decker AN 2 has been a permanent fixture on the forecourt. In October 2011 it was joined by an MIL-MI-2 helicopter which was built in Poland according to a Russian patent.

Schlebusch ist eine beliebte Wohnlage. Dazu gehören die Waldsiedlung, der Leimbacher Berg sowie die Dörfer Edelrath bzw. Neuenhaus, Hummelsheim und Uppersberg.

Schlebusch is a popular residential area. It includes the Waldsiedlung (forest settlement), the Leimbacher Berg (Leimbach Mountain) and the villages Edelrath/Neuenhaus, Hummelsheim and Uppersberg.

Im Park des Bürgerzentrums.
In the park of the community centre. ▼

Bürgerzentrum Schlebusch. Community centre Schlebusch.

Die in einem Park gelegene einstige Villa Wuppermann ist heute ein Bürgerzentrum und Sitz der Bezirksvertretung III. Heinrich Theodor Wuppermann, Inhaber eines Walz- und Schmiedebetriebs, kaufte die Villa 1885 von dem Mülheimer Tuchfabrikanten Christoph Andreae. Bis zur Veräußerung an die Stadt im Jahr 1987 blieb das Anwesen im Eigentum der Familie Wuppermann. 2008 wurde das Gebäude umfassend renoviert.

The former Villa Wupperman and its park-like grounds are today a community centre and the headquarters of the regional representation III. Heinrich Theodor Wuppermann, owner of a milling and cutting company, bought the villa in 1885 from the Mülheim cloth manufacturer Christoph Andreae. The house remained the property of the Wupperman family until it was sold to the city in 1987. In 2008 the building was completely renovated.

Hingucker auf dem Dach eines Einfamilienhauses in Schlebusch. Interesting features on the roof of a house in Schlebusch.

Rastplatz an der Oulustraße/Bergischen Landstraße. A lay-by on Oulustraße/Bergische Landstraße. ▸

Das Industriemuseum Freudenthaler Sensenhammer ging im Jahr 2005 aus der Sensenfabrik Kuhlmann hervor, die 1987 schließen musste. Besonders attraktiv und spannend sind immer wieder die Schmiedevorführungen. Es finden auch Konzerte, Theateraufführungen und andere kulturelle Veranstaltungen statt.

In 2005 the industrial museum Freudenthaler Sensenhammer emerged from the old Kuhlmann blade-making factory which was forced to close in 1987. The forging demonstrations are always exciting to watch. Concerts, plays and other cultural events also take place here.

Schmieden einer Sensensichel. A hooked sickle being forged. ▸

Pfarrkirche St. Nikolaus. Parish church St. Nikolaus.

Haus Steinbüchel, Herrenhaus. "Haus Steinbüchel", manor house.

Im Jahr 1158 wurde erstmalig ein Ritter Konrad von Steinbüchel erwähnt. Er ist Namensgeber des Ortsteils Steinbüchel. Im Laufe der Jahrhunderte wechselte das Rittergut mehrfach den Eigentümer, 1724 wurde es für den Deutschen Orden erworben. Nach dem Brand des ältesten Gotteshauses, der Kapelle in Fettehenne, förderte der Orden den Neubau der 1737 geweihten Kapelle „St. Johannes von Nepomuk". Außerdem ließ er ein Herrenhaus errichten. Nach der Aufgabe des Hofes Ende 1996 entstanden dort ab 1997 Eigentumswohnungen. Der Grundstein für den Bau der Pfarrkirche St. Nikolaus in Neu-Boddenberg, welche die Kirche neben dem Rittergut ersetzte, wurde 1894 gelegt. Aus der alten Kirche stammen drei Altäre, der Taufstein, der Beichtstuhl und das Missionskreuz von 1788. An sie erinnert ein steinernes Wegekreuz, eines von zehn Kreuzen, an denen seit 1963 die Kreuzwallfahrten am Himmelfahrtstag vorbeiführen.

Knight Konrad of Steinbüchel, from whom the district derives its name, is first mentioned in the history books in 1158. Over the centuries the manor house changed hands many times. In 1724 it was acquired for the Teutonic Order. After a fire in the oldest church, the chapel in Fettehenne, the Order paid for the construction of the chapel of St. John of Nepomuk which was consecrated in 1737. It also commissioned the construction of a manor house. This was sold at the end of 1996, and in 1997 the grounds were used to build privately owned apartments.
The foundation stone of the parish church of St. Nikolaus in Neu-Boddenberg, which replaced the church next to the manor house, was laid in 1894. Three altars, the font, the confessional box and the missionary cross from 1788 originate from the old church. The cross is reminiscent of a stone wayside cross, one of ten crosses which the pilgrims of the cross have passed by on Ascension Day since 1963.

Wegekreuz von 1914. Wayside cross from 1914.

Nepomukkapelle. Nepomuk chapel.

Am Oulusee. At the Oulusee Lake.

Haus Steinbüchel und Wohnpark Steinbüchel. "Haus Steinbüchel" and the Steinbüchel residential park.

In der Nähe von Haus Steinbüchel liegt der Wohnpark Steinbüchel (ehemals Derr-Siedlung) vom Anfang der 1970er-Jahre. – Eine seltene Sportart ist Motoball, wie er beim SV Bergfried in Steinbüchel gespielt wird. Zwei Mannschaften versuchen auf knatternden Motorrädern, einen 1,2 Kilo schweren Ball ins gegnerische Tor zu befördern. Ein Spiel dauert 4 x 20 Minuten und wird jeweils durch eine zehnminütige Pause unterbrochen. Jedes Team besteht aus dem Torwart und acht motorisierten Feldspielern, von denen jeweils vier auf dem Platz sind. Sie werden im fliegenden Wechsel ausgetauscht.

Near Haus Steinbüchel is the Steinbüchel residential park (formerly the Derr settlement) which was built at the beginning of the 1970s. – An unusual sport is "motoball" as played by SV Bergfried in Steinbüchel. Two teams playing on roaring motorbikes try to get a 1.2 kg ball into the goal of the opposing team. A game lasts 4 x 20 minutes with a ten-minute-break between each quarter. Each team consists of a goalkeeper and eight field players on motorbikes. Only four of the field players are on the pitch at any one time and are swapped in and out on the fly.

Motoball beim SV Bergfried.
Motoball at SV Bergfried.

Fußgängerbrücke über die Wupper, A59. *Footbridge over the Wupper, A59.*

Anno 1115 wurde Isaak von Rheindorf, ein ritterlicher Dienstmann des Grafen von Berg, erwähnt. Von 1705 bis 1815 wurde in Rheindorf Schiffszoll erhoben. 1930 schlossen sich Rheindorf, Wiesdorf, Schlebusch und Steinbüchel zur Stadt Leverkusen zusammen. Im alten Stadtkern von Rheindorf findet man in den verwinkelten Sträßchen noch viele historische Häuser, so den Zollhof von 1705 und die „Villa Knöterich", beide in der Unterstraße.

Isaak of Rheindorf, a squire to the Count of Berg, was first mentioned in 1115. From 1705 to 1815 tolls were levied on ships at Rheindorf. In 1930 Rheindorf, Wiesdorf, Schlebusch and Steinbüchel joined together as city of Leverkusen. In the old town centre of Rheindorf you can still find winding alleys and historic houses such as the customs office – built 1705 – and "Villa Knöterich", both in Unterstraße.

Zollhof von 1705. *Customs office from 1705.* ▶

„Haus am Orth" und St. Aldegundis. *"Haus am Orth" and St. Aldegundis.*

Kriegerdenkmal 1914–1918. *War memorial 1914–1918.*

Die 2006 eingeweihte evangelische Hoffnungskirche erhielt im Jahr 2008 ein Kolumbarium
(Nischen) für 194 Urnen.
Die katholische Pfarrkirche St. Aldegundis wurde
schon im 12. Jahrhundert erwähnt. Vermutlich gab
es an dem Platz früher eine heidnische Kultstätte.

In 2008 the Evangelical Hoffnungskirche (Church of
Hope), consecrated in 2006, was fitted with a colum-
barium with space for 194 urns.
The Catholic parish church of St. Aldegundis was
mentioned as early as the 12th century. It is likely
that there used to be a pagan ritual spot on this site.

Evangelische Hoffnungskirche. Evangelical Hoffnungskirche (Church of Hope).

Bergerhof von 1784 und St. Aldegundis. Bergerhof from 1784 and St. Aldegundis.

◄ *Hinter dem Deich duckt sich die Pfarrkirche St. Aldegundis.*
The parish church crouches behind the dyke.

Wuppermündung. The mouth of the Wupper.

Die Wupper fließt südlich von Rheindorf in den Rhein. Bis dahin hat sie eine Strecke von 116,5 Kilometern bei einem Gefälle von rund 400 Metern zurückgelegt. Kurz vor der Mündung nimmt die Wupper das Flüsschen Dhünn auf. Ein Deich schützt den Ort vor Hochwasser.

The Wupper flows south from Rheindorf into the Rhine. By that point it has covered 116.5 kilometres with a drop of around 400 metres. Just before the mouth, the river Dhünn flows into the Wupper. A dyke protects Rheindorf from flooding.

Hitdorf liegt malerisch am Rhein. Der 1151 erstmalig als „Huttorp" erwähnte Ort erhielt im Jahr 1857 das Stadtrecht. 1975 kam er zu Leverkusen. Eine Autofähre führt hinüber nach Köln-Langel.

Um 1840 entstanden mehrere Zündholzfabriken, die mit ihren Erzeugnissen das Rheinland belieferten. Die älteste und größte Zündholzfabrik gehörte Johann Michael Fitzen. Sie wurde 1843, 15 Jahre nach Erfindung des Zündholzes durch den englischen Apotheker John Walker, gegründet und stellte jährlich rund 1,5 Millionen Schachteln her. Im Zuge der Kommunalen Gemeindereform wurde Hitdorf 1975 der westlichste Stadtteil Leverkusens.

Hitdorf is located picturesquely on the Rhine. First mentioned in 1151 as "Huttorp", the village was chartered in 1857. In 1975 Hitdorf was amalgamated into Leverkusen. A car ferry shuttles between Hitdorf and Köln-Langel. In around 1840 many matchstick factories sprung up in the area, supplying the Rhineland with their wares. The oldest and biggest matchstick factory belonged to Johann Michael Fitzen. It was founded in 1843, 15 years after the invention of the match by the English chemist John Walker, and produced around 1.5 million boxes a year. As part of the local government redivision in 1975, Hitdorf became the westernmost part of Leverkusen.

Einer Festung gleicht die romanische Pfarrkirche St. Stephanus. Sie wurde 1887 nach dreijähriger Bauzeit fertiggestellt und prägt seitdem das Bild des Ortes.

The Roman parish church of St. Stephan resembles a fortress. It was completed in 1887 after three years of construction and since then has been a local landmark.

Prachtbauten an der Rheinstraße. Elegant buildings on Rheinstraße.

Hitdorf wurde wiederholt vom Rheinhochwasser heimgesucht. Im Jahr 2010 schloss man deshalb eine 900 Meter lange Uferlücke durch eine Schutzmauer mit mobilen Wänden. Als der Rheinpegel im Januar 2011 die kritische Marke von 8,20 Metern überschritt, wurden die Deichtore eingefügt; die Mauer hielt dem Wasser stand.

Hitdorf was constantly plagued by the Rhine flooding. In 2010 a 900-metre-long gap in the bank was accordingly filled in with a protective, mobile wall. When the level of the Rhine exceeded the critical level of 8.2 metres in January 2011, the gates of the dyke were inserted and the wall kept the water back.

▲ *Morgendlicher Blick nach Köln-Langel. An early morning view, looking towards Köln-Langel.*

Schutzmauer. Flood barrier. ▼

Die Fähre zwischen Hitdorf und Köln-Langel nahm den Betrieb 1962 auf. Suboptimale Beschilderung und fehlerhafte Navigationssoftware trugen dazu bei, dass mehrere Fahrzeuge in Langel ungebremst in den Rhein fuhren. Im Oktober 2011 war der Tod eines ortsunkundigen LKW-Fahrers aus Schwelm zu beklagen.

The ferry between Hitdorf and Köln-Langel has been running since 1962. Inadequate signage and erroneous navigation software led many vehicles on the Langel side of the Rhine to drive into the river at full speed. In October 2011, a lorry driver from Schwelm who wasn't familiar with the area drowned in this manner.

Biergarten „Zur Fähre". *The "Zur Fähre" beer garden.*

Fährbetrieb zwischen Hitdorf und Köln-Langel. The ferry between Hitdorf and Köln-Langel.

Der Hafenkran von 1928 wurde 1984 unter Denkmalschutz gestellt. Aus ihm entstand ein ungewöhnliches Café, das Krancafé – wie man sieht, mit Selbstbedienung.

The harbour crane from 1928 was given monument status in 1984. It has been turned into an unusual self-service café, the Krancafé (Crane Café).

Mit dem 1961 von der DEMAG
gebauten Hebekran können die
Boote im Yachthafen zu Wasser
gelassen oder herausgehoben werden.

The hoisting crane, built by DEMAG
in 1961, is used to lower boats in the
yacht harbour into the water.

Wegekreuz von 1703.
Wayside cross from 1703.

Katholische Pfarrkirche St. Maria Rosenkranzkönigin (1914).
Catholic parish church of St. Mary Queen of the Rosary (1914).

Quettingen hieß um 1209 „Quettinheim". Es wurde 1930 zusammen mit Lützenkirchen nach Opladen eingemeindet und kam 1975 zu Leverkusen. Zu Quettingen gehört das Gewerbegebiet Fixheide.

In around 1209 Quettingen was known as "Quettinheim". In 1930 it became part of Opladen along with Lützenkirchen and in 1975 it became part of Leverkusen. The Fixheide business park belongs to Quettingen.

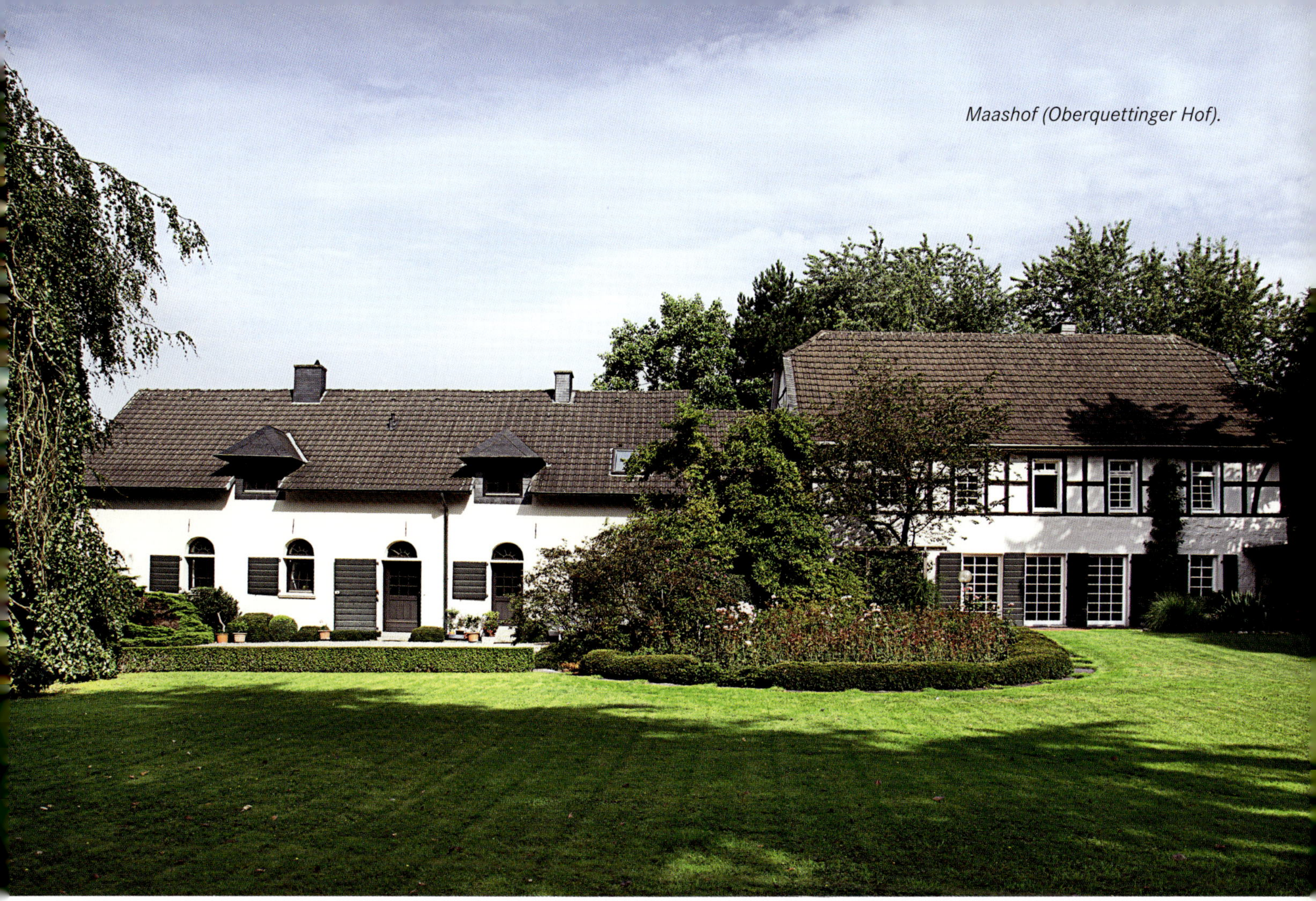

Maashof (Oberquettinger Hof).

Die Biesenbacher Mühle wurde schon 1506 urkundlich erwähnt. Das Foto von 1924 entstand vor dem nicht mehr vorhandenen Gesindehaus. Der Betrieb wurde längst eingestellt.

The Biesenbacher Mill was mentioned in a deed dating back to 1506. The photo was taken in 1924 in front of the servant's quarters which no longer exist. The operation has long since closed down.

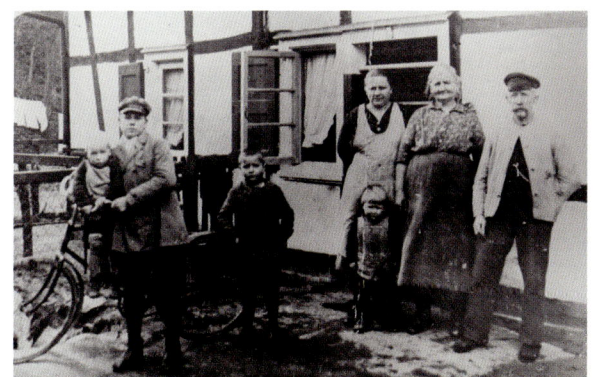

Vor dem Gesindehaus. In front of the servants' quarters.

Evangelische Kirche Bergisch Neukirchen. Evangelical church Bergisch Neukirchen.

Neukirchen wurde schon im 9. oder 10. Jahrhundert besiedelt. Zum Ort gehört u.a. das Dorf Pattscheid (nächste Doppelseite). In einer Urkunde für das Kölner Stift St. Gereon wurde 1223 erstmalig „eine Kirche in Neukirchen" erwähnt, die heutige evangelische Kirche. Das Kirchenschiff wurde 1784 erneuert; die Turmhaube datiert von 1911.

Neukirchen was settled as long ago as the 9th or 10th century. The village of Pattscheid (see next double page) belongs to Bergisch Neukirchen. "A church in Neukirchen" was first mentioned in a deed belonging to the Cologne-based foundation of St. Gereon, dated 1223. This is today's Evangelical church. The nave was renovated in 1784, and the roof of the tower dates back to 1911.

Kirchentür. *Church door.*

Denkmal aus dem Jahr 1911 für die Gefallenen der Kriege von 1815 und 1870/71.

A war memorial from 1911 commemorating those who died in the wars of 1815 and 1870/71.

Der 1991 stillgelegte Bahnhof Pattscheid wurde 1902 für die Strecke Opladen–Remscheid in Betrieb genommen. Er dient heute der illi & Compagnie GmbH als Konferenzzentrum.

Pattscheid station was opened in 1902 serving the Opladen-Remscheid route and was closed in 1991. Today it is a conference centre belonging to illi & Compagnie GmbH.

Wasserturm. Water tower.

Neben der Bergisch Neukirchener Feuerwehr steht der alte denkmalgeschützte zwölf Meter hohe Wasserturm.

Next to the Bergisch Neukirchen fire station is the old, twelve-metre-high water tower which is under a preservation order.

◄ *Bahnhof Pattscheid. Pattscheid station.*

75

Die Gaststätte „Zur Post" (hier der schöne Fachwerkteil) liegt wie die evangelische Kirche im Zentrum von Bergisch Neukirchen.

The "Zur Post" restaurant (the beautiful half-timbered part of which is shown in the picture) is located in the centre of Bergisch Neukirchen along with the Evangelical church.

Gaststätte „Zur Post". The "Zur Post" restaurant.

Die Grunder Kornmühle von 1799 ist dem Verfall preisgegeben. Sie teilt das Schicksal vieler Wind- und Wassermühlen, die in der zweiten Hälfte des 20. Jahrhunderts vor den Großmühlen kapitulieren mussten.

The Grunder corn mill from 1799 has fallen into disrepair. It shares the fate of many windmills and watermills which had to yield to the competition generated by the industrial mills of the 20th century.

Grunder Kornmühle. Grunder corn mill.

Kölner Franziskaner erbauten 1698 die barocke Lützenkirchener Annakapelle. Wegen Baufälligkeit sollte sie zwar wiederholt abgerissen werden, wurde aber dann 1870, 1914 und 1930 restauriert.

In 1698 the Franciscan monks from Cologne built the Baroque Annakapelle. It was due to be torn down when it fell into disrepair but instead was renovated in 1870, 1914 and 1930.

Die alte Maurinuskirche (links, erbaut 1683–1686) und die neue (1844–1847).
The old Maurinuskirche (left, built in 1683–1686) and the new (1844–1847).

Kreuzkapelle. The "Kreuzkapelle".

Kreuz an der Annakapelle.
The cross on the "Annakapelle".

Ohne die Menschen, die mich freundlich beraten haben, wäre es mir nicht möglich gewesen, Leverkusen vorzustellen, denn ich habe dort nie gewohnt oder gearbeitet. Bald stellte ich fest, dass es unmöglich ist, alle Sehenswürdigkeiten der attraktiven Stadt auf 80 Seiten zu zeigen. Deshalb bitte ich um Nachsicht, wenn Sie das eine oder andere vermissen.

Meine Frau Ute beriet mich bei der Gestaltung des Buches. Mein erstes Dankeschön gilt deshalb ihr. Michael Wilde vom Presseamt der Stadt, Andreas Born von der Internet Initiative Leverkusen e.V., Karl Heinz Fröhlingsdorf aus Bergisch Gladbach und Sarah Elizabeth Zollmarsch von der Presseabteilung des Bayer-Konzerns danke ich für ihre Beratung.

Der Luftsportclub Bayer Leverkusen unterstützte mich dankenswerterweise bei meinen Aufnahmen vom Flugplatzfest 2011. Dessen Mitglied Dieter Keienburg steuerte zwei schöne Luftaufnahmen und zusätzliche Informationen zu Haus Steinbüchel bei. In guter Erinnerung bleibt mir auch der Imam der Moschee der Albanischen Gemeinde in Küppersteg, Amir Dzegladini. Das helle Bauwerk mit der glänzenden Kuppel hatte es mir seit Längerem angetan. Ein Anruf öffnete mir schon am nächsten Tag die Türen. Das Ehepaar Schmitz aus Biesenbach glaste ein 1924 vor der früheren Biesenbacher Mühle aufgenommenes Foto ihrer Vorfahren für die Reproduktion aus. Auch andere Menschen, die ich befragte, waren stets freundlich und hilfsbereit. An der ARAL-Tankstelle in Alkenrath mit ihren Fluggeräten war ich mehrmals; der Inhaber, Thomas Spehar, sorgte schließlich für die beste Beleuchtung.

Viele Leverkusener haben so zum Gelingen des Bildbandes beigetragen. Ich wünsche mir, dass er allen Lesern so viel Freude macht, wie ich sie während meiner Streifzüge empfunden habe. Leverkusen ist eine liebenswerte und äußerst interessante Stadt!

Detlef Braun

Without the help of those who advised me, I would never have been able to write about Leverkusen as I have never lived or worked there. I soon realised that it was going to be impossible to mention all the sites of this attractive city on just 80 pages. Therefore please forgive me for any omissions.

My initial thanks go to my wife Ute who helped me design the book. I would like to thank Michael Wilde from the Leverkusen public relations office, Andreas Born from the Internet Initiative Leverkusen e.V., Karl Heinz Fröhlingsdorf from Bergisch Gladbach and Sarah Elizabeth Zollmarsch from the PR Department of the Bayer Group for their help and advice.

Thank you to the Luftsportclub Bayer Leverkusen who allowed me to take photos at the air field fete in 2011. One of the members, Dieter Keienburg, contributed two beautiful aerial photos and also provided additional information about Haus Steinbüchel.

I will always have fond memories of meeting Amir Dzegladini, the imam of the mosque for the Albanian community in Küppersteg. I have long been fascinated by the bright building and its shining dome, and all it took to arrange a visit was one telephone call.

Thanks to Mr. and Mrs. Schmitz from Biesenbach, who removed an old photo of their forbears, taken in 1924 in front of the Biesbach mill, from its frame for reproduction here. Other people I talked to were all very friendly and helpful. I often visited the ARAL petrol station and its flying machines – after all, the owner, Thomas Spehar, arranged the best lighting conditions.

Many people from Leverkusen have contributed to this book and I hope that everyone who reads it will enjoy it as much as I enjoyed putting it together. Leverkusen is a very interesting and likeable city!

Detlef Braun

Bergisch Gladbach

Bilder einer Stadt

Detlef Braun

ISBN: 978-3-86680-901-7 | 14,95 € [D]

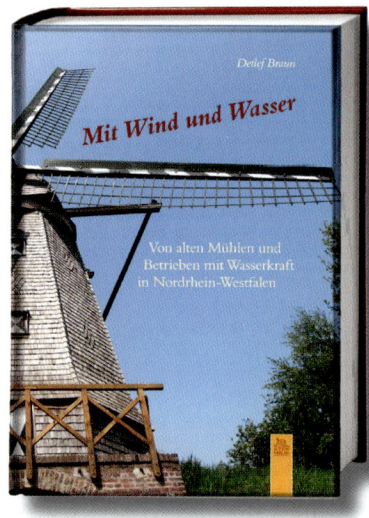

Mit Wind und Wasser.

Von alten Mühlen und Betrieben mit Wasserkraft
in Nordrhein-Westfalen

Detlef Braun

ISBN: 978-3-86680-533-0 | 19,90 € [D]

Entdeckungsreise durch das Bergische Land

18 Tagestouren

Detlef Braun

ISBN: 978-3-86680-832-4 | 14,95 € [D]

Weitere Bücher finden Sie unter:
www.suttonverlag.de

SUTTON
VERLAG